£3

SMT

D1336549

THE PEAK

THE PEAK

A PARK FOR ALL SEASONS

Brian Redhead

Photographs by Ray Manley

Peak National Park

Constable London

First published in Great Britain 1989
by Constable and Company Limited
10 Orange Street London WC2H 7EG
and the Peak Park Joint Planning Board
Copyright © Brian Redhead 1989
Photographs © Peak Park Joint Planning Board 1989
Set in Monophoto Photina 11pt by
BAS Printers Limited, Over Wallop, Hampshire
Printed in Great Britain by
Richard Clay Limited, Bungay, Suffolk

British Library CIP data
Redhead, Brian
The Peak a park for all seasons.
1. England. Peak District. National parks.
Peak District National Park.
I. Title   II. Peak District National Park
719′.32′0942511

ISBN 0 09 468910 5

Design by Karen Sayer

CONTENTS

THE GREAT ESCAPE

I would like to live in the Peak Park without having to move. The house in which I live is one lane west of the Park boundary, or, as I prefer to put it, the Park boundary is one lane east of where I live. And it should move.

When I unveiled the millstone in the centre of our village which marks the entry to the Peak Park, I suggested then that we should move it west to the village boundary but it is not downhill all the way and no one fancied pushing that stone uphill. I shall have to have a word with the Boundary Commissioner.

There was more immediate sympathy for my suggestion that the main road through the village, the road into the Park, should be a B road. Indeed the Parish Council beat me to it.

The road had collapsed, as the locals said it would. It used to be a B road – narrow, twisting and hilly. Then they made it an A road – narrow, twisting and hilly. The locals told the county highways authority that it would never take the weight of the traffic, but the authority would not listen.

First the narrow hump-backed bridge into the next village gave way, then the road into our village began to fall into the field at the end of our lane. All winter and beyond they toiled, at considerable public expense, building buttresses to shore up the road. The local joiner calls it the viaduct, and it took more than a year to construct.

Someone in the village hung a sign on the contractor's hut saying *Happy Birthday*, so you can see that we should be in the Park.

I first set my eyes on the Peak District on a Saturday, and I was working. It was in July 1954, and I had joined the reporting staff of the *Manchester Guardian* the previous Monday. It was the day meat came off the ration and my first assignment was to go to the meat market, where I reported that the return to private enterprise created chaos and panic. There was no bidding. The wholesalers named their prices and the retailers simply shouted their assent.

That night I went to the Palace Theatre where Lena Horne topped the bill, and the last act before the interval was a ventriloquist who began by saying: 'So that you will know that it is me speaking, I shall move my lips.' His name was Harry Worth.

In that heady week I saw Cyril Washbrook in Cross Street, caught a glimpse of John Barbirolli in the foyer of the Midland Hotel, met a window cleaner who sounded like Al Read, and shared digs with a morphologist with whom I subsequently attempted to write a science-fiction novel. It came to nothing.

On the Saturday I went to Buxton.

I went by train and I could not believe what I was seeing through the carriage windows. I had crossed the Pennines by train before, on the Leeds, Huddersfield, Stalybridge and Manchester line, so I knew a Pennine town when I saw one. But this was different. Even from train level, which is not to be compared with riding the roads let alone with scaling the heights, I saw at once that this was like nowhere else.

I had seen more remote places – the

Cheviots as a child; I had seen more beautiful places – the Lake District as an evacuee; I had seen more exotic places – the Far East as a National Serviceman; but I had never before been so taken by surprise by a landscape. One minute I was in the suburbs of Manchester and the next in this most open of open countryside.

And from that day to this, whenever I drive up into the Peak I never fail to get that same feeling of surprise at being so suddenly on top of the world. To live on the edge of the Peak, in Sheffield or in Derby, in Stockport or in Manchester, and, of course, in Macclesfield, is to have delight on your doorstep. It is the great escape.

On that first Saturday I was in Buxton to report a speech to an audience of teachers by J. Chuter Ede, a Labour politician of great wisdom and charm. Back in the office on the Sunday afternoon I wrote my report, which in the tradition of the *Manchester Guardian* was as much about me as about him, and then I held forth in the reporters' room about the wonders of the Peak.

The Deputy Editor, P.J. Monkhouse, was in charge that night and hearing my innocent enthusiasm invited me into his room, once the leaders were safely set, and told me that the Peak was a Park. He was too modest to mention that his book *On Foot in the Peak*, published more than twenty years earlier, was one of the great manifestos of the outdoor movement, and it was only later that I discovered that he was a founder member of the Peak Park Board.

But I swiftly learned that the *Manchester Guardian* was the house journal of the National Park movement, to such an extent that when leader writers were stuck for a final sentence on any subject they were always tempted to write: 'But the situation on the Peak Park Board is acute.'

Years later when I succeeded Paddy as Northern Editor of the *Guardian*, I too added my pen to the debate, but in those early days in Cross Street I was more concerned to explore the place as distinct from the arguments.

At the end of that July my wife of a few weeks arrived in Manchester from Newcastle, having completed her teaching term in order to qualify for her holiday pay. She had £38 10s, and with it we bought our first car.

It was a 1932 two-seater Rover convertible. At least that was what it had been but, when we bought it, it had neither seats nor hood. However we had it fitted with an old bus seat and a pram hood (there was no MOT in those days) and off we went to explore the Peak.

The roads were quieter then than they are now. The serious walkers still arrived by train, and even those out for a run in the car on a Sunday parked and walked; they did not just park and eat.

We, I confess, roared along the roads, making a noise which I would deplore now. The Rover had a six-cylinder engine and a deep-throated exhaust which made it sound both more powerful and faster than it was. It also had a strange transmission system with a worm drive, and any careless use of the clutch could break a half-shaft – which was why I always carried two spares.

But if we rushed up every valley from Longdendale to Dovedale, we also stopped and looked – at Chatsworth and Haddon Hall, at the caves and the caverns, at Mam Tor and Axe Edge, at Ashbourne and Bakewell, at Edale and Eyam.

There was it seemed no end to it. We came to understand, as everyone who knows the Peak comes to understand, that you can go there every weekend of your life and not exhaust it. It is not a place to visit now and then; it is a place to enjoy always.

I think of it as not belonging to some category called leisure but as part of living. And it must always have been like that. A few months ago I opened the remarkable new gallery at Buxton Museum which is called 'Wonders of the Peak', where in a tiny space they have managed to demonstrate that the Peak is an occupied territory and always has been.

It is not a place set aside for occasional enjoyment. There were dinosaurs down the road, and Man has been there since he first stood upright – which is all the more reason both for enjoying it now, and for taking great care of it.

I began to understand that, even in the days when I rushed about in that red Rover. The Peak is not only beautiful to behold, it is fascinating to explore. People who have never visited it always look puzzled when you tell them that it is interesting. That is not the adjective they expect. Wild, yes. Beautiful, yes. Bleak, even. But interesting?

The answer is hugely so, which is why so many people take up the cause of the Peak, not simply to protect it and to allow access to it, but to treasure it. They want it used, but not abused. They want people to know it for what it is: a landscape that is both geography and history, naturally beautiful but also inhabited. 'Keep Out' signs have no place in the Park, but, as I constantly repeat, it is not enough to say there must be access without adding access to do what.

The Peak is like anything we value. It has to be looked after.

In the January of 1955, I remember, I was dispatched with a photographer to the Peak – the same man who had once been heard to say in the Free Trade Hall in Manchester: 'Just pretend to be playing the violin, Mr Menuhin.' We went to report on the farmers' plight in the snow.

As we failed to get stuck in a snowdrift, I decided that there was no story. 'There had better be,' said Mr Cockburn, the news editor, 'because there is a column on page seven to be filled.'

I struggled but I succeeded. 'The sheep', I wrote, 'are still out on the hills around High Peak. The snow is not yet deep enough to bury them, and because fodder is scarce the farmers are leaving them out as long as they dare.'

We had found one farmer, Oliver Archer, whose farm was about two miles from the Snake Pass, and had been cut off from the main road for two days. He was taking his milk to the road by horse and sledge. And so I wrote on, finishing at the Cat and Fiddle, high up between Macclesfield and Buxton, where the sunlight suddenly vanished in a thick mist.

'There you are,' said Co, as we called him, 'there is always a story in the Peak.' To which he ought to have added, 'if you write for the *Manchester Guardian*.'

I began to write many stories about the Peak. I wrote about the last ropemaker at Castleton. His name was Bert Marrison and when he died, not so long ago, his ashes were buried along with some of his tackle in the Peak Cavern where he had worked for so many years.

I spent a night in the railway tunnel at Dove Holes and wrote a piece which began: 'The last train to enter Dove Holes Tunnel at night stays there till morning. It is the tunnel train, a mobile building unit, drawn by a diesel engine.'

It had to be diesel because the brick lining of the tunnel which had been cut through the limestone ninety years previously had been continuously eroded by sulphuric fumes from the locomotives. The re-lining took three years, as I recall. Dove Holes Tunnel served the main line from Manchester Central to London St Pancras, and was far and away the finest route to London precisely because it allowed you a glimpse of the Peak.

I also had my first car crash on a journey through the Peak. Not in the Rover but in a company car which the reporters had just won permission to use. It was a Morris Oxford. I was on my way from Manchester to Hull to cover the campaign there in the 1955 general election. Naturally I chose to go via the Peak. I drove up Longdendale, past the house where L.S. Lowry lived, and where I was later to interview him. He told me, I remember, that his favourite piece of music was Bellini's *Norma*.

I successfully negotiated Woodhead and Penistone but just as I was coming to Hoyland Swaine, I failed to complete a left-hand bend. I bounced off a car coming the other way, and just before my car went through a stone wall, I rolled on to the floor. There was a lot of room between the front bench seat and the dashboard on that model. The car demolished the wall and much of itself, but I emerged with only a bruise and a scratch.

The general manager at the *Manchester Guardian*, Mr Markwick, was not amused, especially when he got the bill for rebuilding the drystone wall, an expense I would be much in favour of these days. The editor on the other hand, the great A.P. Wadsworth, took a more sanguine view of the incident. 'Hello Stirling Moss,' he said, when he next saw me, and promptly appointed me Motoring Correspondent.

I now had a choice of cars in which to explore the Peak and places far beyond. I drove a Rolls-Royce, I remember, from Crewe to Beaulieu, where Lord Montagu was thinking of starting his Motor Museum.

I drove, or rather was driven, by Stirling Moss himself in the first Austin Healey from Cannes to Nice. He went so fast along the upper Corniche that at one point three men who were sitting on a wall fell off backwards in sheer astonishment as we sped past.

I even drove a double-decker bus through Manchester.

But circumstances were taking me away from the Park. Babies arrived, and we no longer rushed about as much. I got stuck behind a desk in the office, commissioning

pieces instead of composing them. And the motorways arrived.

Almost my last assignment as Motoring Correspondent was to cover the opening of the Preston by-pass, Britain's first motorway. The Friends of the M6 came much later. But there were new routes spreading north and south and new train services which ignored the old Central Line, and suddenly I was either travelling north to the Lakes or south to London but never across the Peak.

Until one Boxing Day.

After three years living in London we had returned to Manchester in 1965 for me to succeed Paddy Monkhouse, and when the children announced that they fancied a real walk, we went up Kinder. The mist descended and we didn't. We got lost, and after going round and round in circles for what seemed like an eternity but was probably all of forty minutes, and passing Noe Stool three times, we were rescued by a Park Warden.

But the Peak was once more part of daily life. First in the pages of the *Guardian*, then in the *Manchester Evening News*, and after that for BBC Television in the North West, I had the opportunity both to write about the Peak again and to explore it once more.

It was even more fascinating than I had remembered. I found every excuse to visit Chatsworth again and Haddon Hall, to pause and look at Ashford-in-the-Water, to explain to the viewers in the North West, and subsequently to the nation on 'Today', that a Bakewall tart is not a tart but a pudding.

I stood under an umbrella high on the hills and explained for television why the clouds that blow across the Atlantic deposit their water on these hills and what happens to it next. And when Manchester was robbed of its powers as a water authority I wrote an indignant article entitled 'On the water affront'.

I told an American radio audience all about

Ashbourne, its water and its football match on Shrove Tuesday. I told them too about Buxton water and Buxton Spa, about the Dukes of Devonshire, and about Cromford and Richard Arkwright. Americans are very fond of Arkwright. They like people who can boast that they made enough money in twenty years personally to wipe out the national debt.

I interviewed people all over the Peak, from Foolow to Grindleford, from Tideswell to Tintwistle. I even got the opportunity, which I had long wished for, to tell again the tale of Eyam. It may have been told a thousand times, but I hope it goes on being told on the last Sunday in August every year forever.

It is a story of self-sacrifice without equal, of a tiny village sealing itself off from the world so that no one else would suffer as they suffered from the imported plague. No fewer than 259 people from 76 families died in Eyam after George Viccars, in all innocence, brought the plague from London, and no hero is more tragic than William Mompesson, the young vicar who united the village in its courage and then buried his own wife in August 1666.

For seven years I made a series of television programmes for BBC North West called 'Homeground', which were about the geography and the history of this part of England. But only part of the Peak is part of the North West in terms of television transmitters, and I could venture into it only occasionally with cameras.

I had the same problem with Haworth. In television terms it is embraced from Leeds not Manchester. But I could not resist telling the story of the hapless curate there who preceded Patrick Brontë. The villagers took a dislike to the young man and tormented him in church on three successive Sundays. When the local chimneysweep, who was drunk, embraced him in the pulpit and showered him with soot, the curate decided he had had enough and fled. His name was Samuel Redhead.

Buxton I always believed was firmly in our embrace, and the restoration of the Opera House, accompanied by the start of the Buxton Festival, was a great excuse to make a song and dance about the place. Buxton is not in the Park but surrounded by it, and going to and from the opera there on the Cat and Fiddle road is one of the joys of life.

It was at a party in Buxton on the opening night of one of the Festivals that the then Secretary to the Cabinet, a man who was later to admit to being economical with the truth, solemnly assured me that Buxton was as far north as he ever ventured. That figures, I thought.

In 1986 I was invited to become President of the Council for National Parks. I accepted and found myself in the politics of the Parks and of the Peak. The first thing I discovered was how little I knew about the Peak and the Parks compared with people like Michael Dower, the Park Officer, and Roland Smith, the Head of Information Services, with whom I have worked on this book.

And I was not alone. Others too had come to realize how little they knew and how little was known, which was why a National Parks awareness campaign was launched. The principal event was a Festival at Chatsworth in 1987 where I took the opportunity to make clear what I felt needed to be said about the Parks – their purpose, their protection, and their future.

As a result of this new involvement my attitude to the Peak has not so much changed as sharpened. I treasure its every acre even more. I take every opportunity to enjoy it, if only as an alternative route on a car journey.

Given the choice between a motorway and a road through the Park, I settle for the latter. I drive to London not down the M6 any more, but from Buxton to Ashbourne and then through Derby on the A52 to the M1. I don't go to Leeds on the M62 but through Glossop and past Hoyland Swaine to the M1.

Going or coming, a journey through the Peak is a refreshment for the soul. If I go to Sheffield I go there and back through Winnats Pass. And the journey from our village to the next, Kettleshulme, which I travel countless times, never ceases to delight me.

I applaud when I hear that heather is being planted by helicopter on Kinder. I was overjoyed to be invited to unveil the restoration of Jacob's Ladder, where young men had constructed a new stone staircase with stones pulled from the river bed to cover the scar of many thousands of feet. It looked, I said at the time, like an Iron Age excavation.

But all the time there is the nagging fear that the volume of visitors, including me going hither and thither by car, is too much for the Peak. I even wondered out loud whether the Pennine Way itself ought to be closed to pedestrians for a year or two to give it a chance to recover from the erosion by all those feet. But I was talked out of it.

I sympathize with the people of Stoney Middleton whose lives are made a misery by the thunder of heavy traffic through their village. I question the wisdom of erecting signposts which point traffic though the Park to one motorway or another, even though I take the short cut myself.

I sympathize with those villagers in the Park who do not want some great leisure centre which will distort their village, but I sympathize, too, with those local residents who seek new work.

The Peak is a working Park, that is its special character. Because of what it is and where it is, it cannot be seen as an occasional place. Its management is not a fringe activity, it is a full-time job. For the professional it is about work not leisure, about employment not recreation. It is a serious business, and it cannot be left to chance.

It is, I am fond of saying, peace not war. War is dramatic, noisy, damaging – like the threats to the National Park. The good things are gentle, quiet, conserving, but you have to work at them.

The Peak cannot be protected or enhanced by doing nothing. That is not conservation, that is neglect. The quiet work must go on (and it is a great employer) so that everyone can continue to enjoy the Peak.

It is perhaps too easy, especially if you get sight of the Planning Board papers and enter the arguments, to concentrate only on the struggle and to forget the joy. The reward is all around us.

I emerged one night, I recall, after a bruising encounter at Losehill Hall, where I had not won all the arguments, and drove off into the moonlight. After one scowl at the cement works, which must be the most beautifully sited eyesore in the world, I drove through Castleton past Peveril Castle and Speedwell Cavern, through Winnats and down Rushup Edge, home. Why, I asked myself, are you so agitated when there is all this to enjoy?

Two days later I got the answer – a celebration of a famous battle to enjoy it. It was a Sunday in April and a very special anniversary. A large number of quite elderly people gathered in a quarry in the Peak and sang their old battle song:

I'm a rambler, I'm a rambler
from Manchester way;
I get all my pleasure
the hard moorland way;
I may be a wage slave
on Monday,
But I am a freeman on Sunday.

The singers, most of whom had long ceased to be wage slaves, and many of whom could only ramble a step or two, had gathered to celebrate the Kinder Trespass, the mass act of defiance which began from that same quarry in 1932.

Beneath a permanent plaque which records that the Mass Trespass of Kinder Scout started from Bowden Bridge Quarry a mile out of Hayfield, the leader of that Trespass, Benny Rothman, addressed the gathering. He told the story of that day – the trespass on the forbidden moorland, the fights with the gamekeepers, the arrests by the police. Benny was one of the five who subsequently went to prison.

Almost everyone in that audience already knew the story of that famous day (all ramblers do) and not everyone of those assembled approved. Some think the Trespass was a great irrelevance. They said so at the time and they argue with Benny still.

But others, and I am one, think it must have concentrated minds wonderfully. It laid claim to a right, a right then denied but soon after to be conceded (at least in principle). And hearing Benny tell it again was not only to relive the argument but to see its justice.

Later in the pub, speaker after speaker applauded the original trespassers (twenty of whom were present) and then went on to categorize the present threats to the Peak and the obstacles to access – the indiscriminate planting of conifers, the privatization of water, inappropriate tourist developments.

They talked too of the problems that the access won has brought – eighteen and a half million visitors a year in the Peak Park alone.

'Forgive us our Trespass,' said one old gentleman, with mock contrition. But he fooled no one, because everyone present knew that the days that they had enjoyed most in their lives had been spent in the Peak Park. And they want succeeding generations to continue to enjoy it.

They knew, as I know, that the Peak is a Park for all seasons, not just for the holiday season; a Park for all seasons of the calendar; a Park for people of all ages, and for all ages of mankind.

The Peak embraces both those who live in its shadow and those who live in its midst. And when they lift their eyes to these hills, all people rejoice.

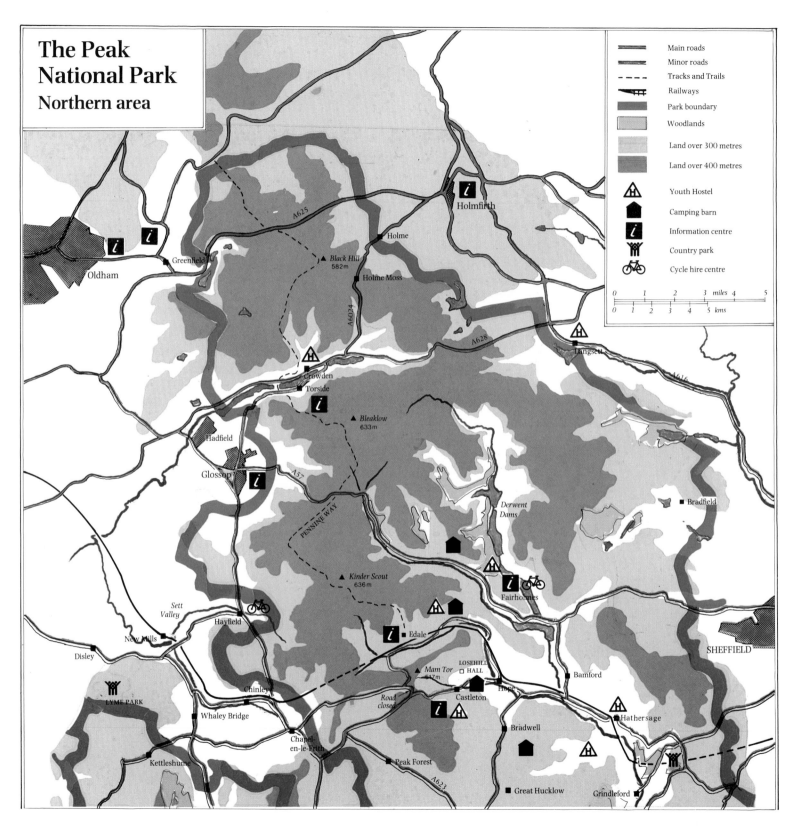

The Peak National Park
Northern area

Legend:
- Main roads
- Minor roads
- Tracks and Trails
- Railways
- Park boundary
- Woodlands
- Land over 300 metres
- Land over 400 metres
- Youth Hostel
- Camping barn
- Information centre
- Country park
- Cycle hire centre

0 1 2 3 miles 4 5
0 1 2 3 4 5 kms

Holmfirth

Holme

Oldham

Greenfield

Black Hill
582m

Holme Moss

A625

A6024

A628

Langsett

A616

Crowden

Torside

Bleaklow
633m

Hadfield

Glossop

A57

PENNINE WAY

Derwent Dams

Bradfield

Kinder Scout
636m

Fairholmes

Sett Valley

Hayfield

New Mills

Disley

Edale

SHEFFIELD

Mam Tor
517m

LOSEHILL HALL

Castleton

Hope

Bamford

Chinley

Road closed

Bradwell

Hathersage

LYME PARK

Whaley Bridge

Chapel-en-le-Frith

Kettleshume

Peak Forest

A623

Great Hucklow

Grindleford

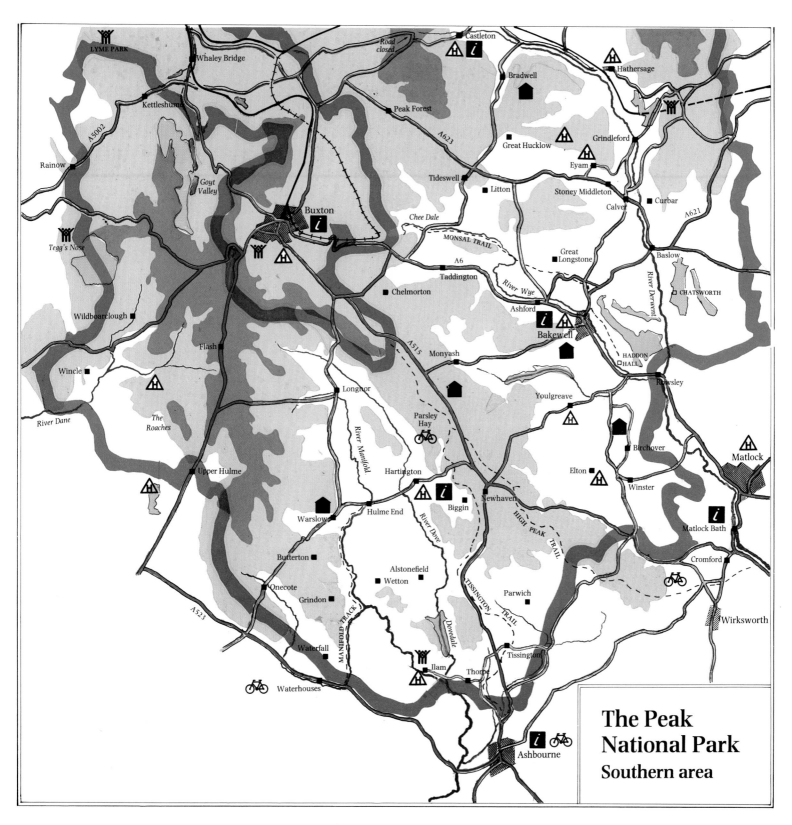

LYME PARK

Whaley Bridge

Kettleshulme

Rainow

A5002

Goyt
Valley

Tegg's Nose

Wildboarclough

Flash

Wincle

River Dane

The
Roaches

Upper Hulme

Warslow

Butterton

Onecote

Grindon

A523

Waterfall

Waterhouses

Road
closed

Peak Forest

A623

Buxton

Chee Dale

MONSAL TRAIL

A6

Taddington

Chelmorton

Ashford

A515

Monyash

Longnor

River Manifold

Parsley
Hay

Hartington

Hulme End

Alstonefield

Wetton

MANIFOLD TRACK

River Dove

Dovedale

Ilam

Thorpe

Ashbourne

Castleton

Hathersage

Bradwell

Great Hucklow

Grindleford

Eyam

Tideswell

Litton

Stoney Middleton

Calver

Curbar

A621

Great
Longstone

River Wye

Bakewell

HADDON
HALL

Baslow

River Derwent

CHATSWORTH

Rowsley

Youlgreave

Birchover

Elton

Winster

Matlock

Newhaven

HIGH PEAK TRAIL

Biggin

Parwich

TISSINGTON TRAIL

Tissington

Matlock Bath

Cromford

Wirksworth

**The Peak
National Park**
Southern area

15

SPRING

Spring comes late to the moors and the dales of the Peak District. Snow shadows linger long in the lee of the sinuous miles of patiently constructed drystone walls which enmesh the rolling landscape like a net.

The walls, largely monuments to eighteenth- and nineteenth-century enclosures, contain fields filled with the sounds of new-born lambs, whose mothers were brought down from the high moors to give birth. It is the start of the age-old farming cycle, a time of rebirth and new beginnings.

Nature too reawakens from her long winter sleep, and the first flowers shyly appear, often to have their petals nipped by a last icy blast of winter. The yellow stars of the celandine are usually the first to show, closely followed by ramsons, wood anemones and a misty carpet of bluebells in the old oak woods.

These flowers are opportunists, blooming quickly before the fresh green leaves start to appear on the trees above. The last of the trees to show its leaves is the lime-loving ash, so characteristic of the White Peak plateau.

Rites of spring

Patient birdwatchers on certain isolated moors
on the western side of the National Park can
be treated to one of the most spectacular
displays in British ornithology. The mating
display, or 'lek', of the black grouse is a frenetic
affair between blackcocks, with much
exaggerated posturing and threat but little
actual contact. Once the pecking order has
been established, the dowdier grey hens
appear and mating takes place.

Mermaid's tale

High on exposed moorland near Warslow lies wind-whipped Blake Mere, a place of mystery and legend. Against the distant backdrop of Hen Cloud and The Roaches, this isolated tarn is said to be the home of a mermaid who lures the young men unfortunate enough to see her to a watery grave. The Mermaid pub further along the ridge celebrates the legend with a more palatable drink.

A watery rarity

Waterfalls are not common on the Peak, but
these pretty cascades in Crowden Great Brook,
Longdendale, are among the most delightful,
falling over emerald mosses into a rocky gorge
in the gritstone moor. The Pennine Way starts
its second stage from Crowden up this remote
and beautiful valley.

The Booths of Edale

The valley of Edale is punctuated by a string of farming hamlets known as 'booths', meaning a temporary shelter originally named by Tudor herdsmen. Edale village is thus more correctly known as Grindsbrook Booth, after the deep valley which comes down from the crag-rimmed heights of Kinder Scout and which now carries the Pennine Way. The others are Upper Booth, Barber Booth, Ollerbrook Booth and finally Nether Booth, at the eastern end of the valley.

The twins

Spring is harvest-time for Peak shepherds,
when the new 'crop' of lambs appears. Twins,
like those seen here, are a special bonus to the
farmer, rewarding months of patient
stockmanship through the long hard days of
winter.

Woodland flowers

One of the joys of walking through woodland
in spring is the sudden appearance of wild
flowers, like these bluebells and wood
stitchworts, seen near Bakewell. The delicate
wood stitchwort is a local rarity, recorded
infrequently in the Park, but there are several
beautiful bluebell woods, especially in the older
sessile oak woods on the gritstone.

An epic sacrifice

Seven graves on a bleak hillside above the
village of Eyam mark the last resting place of
members of the Hancock family, struck down
by the 'visitation' of the plague in 1666.
Within the space of a week, Mrs Hancock had
the sad task of burying her husband and six
children as plague swept through the village
suffering under a self-imposed quarantine
designed to protect the rest of the county. The
Riley Graves, as these poignant memorials are
known, overlook Middleton Dale and the
snow-brushed Longstone Moor beyond.

The other Dovedale

Spring brings a myriad of shades of fresh green
to the limestone dales. The upper reaches of
the Dove, seen here near Drabber Tor (left) in
Wolfscote Dale, never receive the same
number of visitors as the overcrowded lower
stretches, and the walker can often have them
to himself. These precipitous valleys are a fine
place to appreciate the enormous power of the
post-Ice Age meltwater streams which formed
them ten thousand years ago.

Start of a marathon

A misty April morning in Grindsbrook Clough on the southern edge of the Park's highest summit, the 2,088-foot plateau of Kinder Scout. Tom Stephenson's Pennine Way starts its 250-mile trek up England's backbone here, and walkers get their first true taste of upland Britain.

A frog goes a-wooing

The common frog, not so common any more
as wetlands disappear, emerges from its
hibernation to leave its spawning ponds and
live on land during April. Common frogs can
be found on moorland at altitudes of over
1,000 feet in the Peak, where they are less
threatened than on more intensively
cultivated farmland.

Norman outpost

Pilsbury Castle, guarding the valley of the
Upper Dove, is one of the most evocative places
in the White Peak. It is also one of the best-
preserved motte-and-bailey castle sites in the
Park, the double earthworks still standing out
clearly in the sheep-cropped grass and
overlooked by a sentinel limestone crag. The
fortifications are thought to have been built
during the troubled reign of King Stephen.

Beef for market

These piratical-looking black-and-white
Hereford/Friesian calves, pictured near
Wardlow, provide further evidence of the
arrival of spring on the White Peak plateau.
They are reared for their beef and will probably
be sold at the local markets of Bakewell or
Hope.

Angler's delight

A carpet of water crowsfoot covers the gentle
waters of the River Bradford in Bradford Dale,
near Youlgreave. These large expanses of
slower-moving water were created between
weirs to assist breeding fish at a time when
freshwater fish was an important source of
food. Today they are the delight of anglers.

The Salt Cellar

The Salt Cellar is a prominent gritstone tor on
Derwent Edge, overlooking the forested,
reservoir-filled valley of the Upper Derwent in
the north-east of the National Park. These
exotically shaped tors have been sculptured by
wind, rain and frost over millions of years from
the softer rocks which once surrounded them.

The walls walk slowly

Limestone drystone walls on the plateau near Litton. These incredible monuments to man's endeavour are chiefly the result of the Enclosure Movements of the eighteenth and nineteenth centuries, and they spread across the limestone plateau in a gigantic network. Those on the far left 'fossilize' the ancient medieval strip-fields running down to Tansley Dale and Peter's Dale.

'The Vale of Tempe'

Spring sunshine filters through the leafy canopy of a tree overhanging the Wye in Monsal Dale, a valley which John Ruskin described as being 'divine as the Vale of Tempe; you might have seen the Gods there morning and evening – Apollo and all the sweet Muses of the light – walking in fair procession on the lawns of it'.

A barn storm

A springtime storm brews on the White Peak
plateau, and the old field barn prepares to
withstand yet another battering by the
capricious weather. These important features
of the Peak landscape are now often
redundant to the farmers' needs, but some
have been 'rescued' in imaginative schemes
like the Park's camping barns project.

View from the Snake

Spring sun transforms the moorland grass into folds of green velvet in this view of the northern edge of Kinder Scout and Fairbrook Naze from the Snake road.

Ilam Rock

The great 100-foot white fang of limestone
known as Ilam Rock (after the village above)
is only one of many spectacular rock features
in the five-mile walk through the Peak's best-
known dale. Dovedale, made famous by Izaak
Walton and Charles Cotton's *The Compleat
Angler*, remains a popular place for visitors, the
more discerning of whom come outside the
over-crowded summer season.

Sunset over Stanage

Golden evening sunshine lights Back Tor, Lose
Hill and Win Hill, with the Kinder plateau in
the background, in this view from the Stanage
Edge escarpment.

SUMMER

In the shimmering heat of high summer, the limestone crags and walls of the White Peak seem to reflect the sun's rays with an intensity which can sometimes be dazzling.

The sultry stillness is broken only by the occasional distant rumble of thunder coming from the heavy, blue-black clouds which give the local name to the similarly coloured banks of meadow cranesbill, flowering in roadside verges.

These showy blooms are in great demand for the unique Peak custom of well-dressing, a colourful thanksgiving for the gift of life-giving water in this porous landscape. The White Peak in summer is a land of disappearing rivers, and large crowds of visitors are treated to marvellous displays of floral beauty at the well-dressings and, more naturally, in the dales.

The purple-hued heather of the high moorlands of the gritstone Dark Peak is at its best in late summer. After the 'Glorious Twelfth' of August, certain moors are closed as shooting-parties set out in pursuit of Britain's premier game bird, the red grouse. The grouse's staccato 'Go back' still echoes mockingly across the tor-topped heights of the roof of the Peak, sounding a warning to ill-equipped walkers.

Noe Stool, Kinder

Silhouetted dramatically against the summer sky is Noe Stool, one of a series of wind-carved gritstone tors which punctuate the 2,000-foot Kinder Scout plateau. The outcrop takes its name from the River Noe, the main watercourse of the Edale Valley, which rises between here and the brooding escarpment of Swine's Back in the background.

Down in the woodlands

The old sessile oak woods of Padley Gorge,
near Grindleford, are a remnant of the
extensive natural woodland which once
cloaked large areas of the gritstone and shale
Dark Peak. This is an extremely rich habitat
for wildlife – an oak tree can support up to
three hundred different species of insects,
compared with only a handful on the
introduced conifers of the more recent
softwood plantations.

For hay no more

Field barns, like this one near Sheldon, were once an important part of the farming economy, where summer-cut hay was stored to provide vital winter feed for stock. Today, however, silage-making has largely replaced hay-making on Peakland farms, and barns like this, although important as landscape features, are now often redundant to the farmer's needs.

Thunderclouds by the roadside

The showy purple flowers of the meadow
cranesbill are known locally as
'thunderclouds' because they appear in large
banks on roadside verges at the time of
midsummer thunderstorms. Members of the
geranium family, meadow cranesbills get their
official name from their seedheads, which
resemble a crane's bill.

Patterns of the past

This view of the Upper Dove valley, looking towards Nab End with the rolling moors of Axe Edge beyond, clearly shows evidence of medieval 'ridge and furrow' cultivation in the foreground. These linear corrugations mark the passage of oxen teams which were turned at the end of each furrow to create the distinctive 'reversed S' patterns found in these fields.

On the edge

Walking the edges is one of the most popular activities in the Park, and this view of Curbar Edge from Bamford Edge is typical. The gritstone edges form a glorious promenade for about twelve miles down the eastern side of the Park, providing superb views across the broad valley of the Derwent to the limestone plateau beyond.

Guardians of the dale

Seen from the air, the pyramidal mass of
Thorpe Cloud (top) and the gentler slopes of
Bunster Hill (below) stand guard at the
entrance to one of the most famous of the
Peak's dales, Dovedale. Proposed in the 1930s
as a separate National Park, Dovedale, with its
spectacular rock formations carved from the
reef limestomes, suffers from its own
popularity, and urgent remedial works have
been necessary to its main footpaths.

Magpie Mine

Lead-mining was one of the most important industries in the Peak from Roman times until it reached its zenith in the eighteenth century, and the White Peak plateau and dales still bear many marks of the Peak's 'Lead Rush'. The most complete and evocative remains of a lead mine in the Park are at Magpie Mine near Sheldon, which was worked almost continuously for two centuries. The photograph shows the distinctive round 'Cornish' chimney and the remains of the pump house.

Ramshaw ramparts

The serrated skyline of Ramshaw Rocks stands
above the main Leek-Buxton road near Leek.
These strange towers of pinkish gritstone are
a favourite spot for rock scramblers, and the
western view from them extends over the
Cheshire Plain as far as the distant glint of the
River Mersey.

Sylvan study

Trees are an important softening agent in the Peak landscape, and the decline in grazing of the limestone dales has seen a dramatic increase in tree cover compared with that which existed in Victorian times.

Moat Stone, Kinder

On the southern edge of the Kinder Scout
plateau, between Crowden Tower and Noe
Stool, lies an extraordinary collection of
gritstone tors known as the Wool Packs or, in
a reference to their strange animal-like shapes,
Whipsnade. Among them is this isolated block
completely encircled by water, known to
walkers as the Moat Stone.

Monyash

A summer's evening in the White Peak village of Monyash, high on the limestone plateau. The name is thought to mean 'many ash trees'. The village was an important lead-mining centre in the eighteenth century, with its own Barmote Court. In the background the lines of enclosure walls mark the older Saxon strip fields.

Daisies from dereliction

Ox-eye daisies, known locally as moon daisies,
flower alongside the High Peak Trail, a former
railway route which, like the Tissington Trail,
has been converted by the National Park to a
walking and riding track. The High Peak Trail
follows the route of the former Cromford and
High Peak Railway, which was originally
planned as a canal with stations called wharfs,
and opened in 1830.

Approaching storm

Black-faced Suffolk sheep graze peacefully on
the sweet limestone pastures near Wheston,
while the black clouds behind threaten an
approaching summer thunderstorm.

Castles in the air

Alport Castles, just off the Snake road, is the
site of Britain's biggest landslip, where a whole
hillside has collapsed on unstable shales to
create a Wild West wilderness of cliffs, towers
and fallen boulders. The Tower (centre) is a
detached block looking for all the world like a
crenellated Norman keep, and it gives the
place its name.

Minninglow

The spindly crown of ancient beeches on the
windswept summit of Minninglow beside the
High Peak Trail is one of the most prominent
landmarks in the Peak, visible from many high
points. It marks the site of a late-Neolithic
round cairn containing at least four Megalithic
burial chambers, constructed more than four
thousand years ago with an expert eye to the
prominent location.

Featherbedded moors

Many of the northern moors of the Peak take
the name of Featherbed Moss, an unlikely
epithet, at first sight, for these desolate,
chocolate-brown peat bogs. But in early
summer, some poorly drained moors are
transformed with drifts of the fluffy white
flower-heads of cottongrass, looking like tufts
of cotton wool waving in the wind. They were
once used for making candlewicks and for
stuffing pillows and mattresses.

Sheep safely graze

A still summer's evening on the limestone
plateau near Wardlow.

Jewel of summer

A female Common Blue butterfly soaks up the summer sunshine at rest on the grasses of a limestone dale. The Common Blue is the most numerous of the blue butterflies found in the Peak, but the female, shown here, is actually more brown than blue. The main foodplant of this butterfly is bird's-foot trefoil, or 'bacon and eggs', a common plant in the limestone dales of the Peak.

Fair Brook, Kinder Scout

Sheep graze as the last of the heather blooms
in Fair Brook on the northern slopes of Kinder
Scout, looking towards the Snake Road. The
glorious purple of the heather is managed
almost exclusively for the red grouse, which
depends on this wiry shrub for both its bed and
its board. Access agreements, negotiated by
the National Park with moorland owners,
allow walkers freedom to roam except for a
handful of days after the 'Glorious Twelfth' of
August, when grouse-shooting takes place.

AUTUMN

Autumn steals subtly into the cloughs and dales of the Peak, as green turns to gold, russet and red in a colourful climax to the dying year.

It is a great time for walking in the White or Dark Peak, because the area often enjoys an Indian summer of glorious sunny days at this time of the year. Ramblers setting out early enough can experience the sensation of walking above the clouds, as they emerge from the clammy mist of the valley bottom to crisp autumn sunshine on the heights above.

Gradually the sun burns off the mist in these conditions of temperature inversion, and then good days can be spent tramping along the superb promenades created by the Peakland edges of gritstone crags. Dry days can also be dangerous on the Dark Peak moorlands, because the risk of fire is great when the sun bakes the peat tinder-dry.

But as the leaves fall to create a multi-coloured carpet on the dale-side paths, autumn becomes one of the most beautiful times of the year to the true connoisseur of the Peakland scene.

Monsal morning

A fresh autumn morning in Monsal Dale. The
River Wye cascades over a weir constructed to
provide breeding ponds for the trout which
thrive in the clear, unpolluted waters, and
provide sport for anglers who pay large sums
to fish these privileged waters.

Sharks and Dragons

Rising like a shark's fin from the morning mist is the reef limestone peak of Parkhouse Hill in the Upper Dove valley. To the left is its sister peak of Chrome Hill, known locally as 'The Dragon's Back'. These upstanding hills of fossil-rich limestone were formed in reefs during the Carboniferous period three hundred million years ago, and their distinctive shapes are owing to their relative resistance to the timeless forces of erosion.

To market, to market

Tightly huddled into a pen at Bakewell Market, these sheep wait to be sold under the hammer of the fast-talking auctioneer. Market day in Bakewell is a weekly highlight in the Peak's farming calendar – a social as well as a business event. The streets of the little town are filled with hay wagons and cattle floats and the pubs filled with red-faced farmers.

Finger Stone, Ramshaw

Like an umpire's unequivocal finger, this isolated gritstone tor points heavenwards from the weird rock garden of Ramshaw Rocks, on the Staffordshire moorlands east of Leek. This is an area of a multitude of strange rock formations, including one known as the Winking Man, who appears to open and close his 'eye' as the motorist passes beneath on the A53 Leek-Buxton road.

Village focus

There is a strong tradition of proud Non-
conformism in Peakland communities, and the
chapel is usually an important focus for
villagers. This view of the Congregational
Chapel in Tideswell places the building where
it has been for a century – at the very centre
of the community.

Carl Wark

The mysterious fortification known as Carl
Wark, east of Hathersage, has baffled
archaeologists for years. At one time it was
thought to be of Romano-British date, but now
an Iron Age date is usually attributed to its
massive revetted ramparts, which rise above
the glowing bracken of Hathersage Moor.

Tufa dam, Lathkill Dale

Autumn tints the rowan leaves overhanging
the tufa dam at Carter's Mill in Upper Lathkill
Dale. The formation of tufa only occurs in the
purest limestone streams, when calcium
carbonate is deposited over existing mosses
and rocks. Carter's Mill was a corn mill
grinding grain from local farms, and the
Lathkill is the only Peakland river which runs
for its entire length over limestone.

Landscape in the clouds

Keats's 'season of mists' lives up to its name in
this photograph taken from the heights of
Curbar Edge, looking down into the Derwent
valley. Like smoke rising from a thousand
chimneys, mist swirls among the trees and
hedgerows, creating a landscape in the clouds.

Autumn glory

The burnished copper of fallen beech leaves
lights the autumn coolness of Burbage Brook
as it cascades through Padley Gorge near
Grindleford, a property owned and protected
by the National Trust.

Landmark on the Snake

A solitary oak stands sentinel over the Snake
road, Thomas Telford's 1821 turnpike
between Bamford and Glossop, which is often
closed by winter snows. The brooding slopes of
Kinder Scout form the backdrop to this most
dramatic Peakland motor route which rises to
a height of 1,680 feet.

Viator's Bridge, Milldale

'Why!' exclaims Viator in Izaak Walton's classic *The Compleat Angler*, 'a mouse can hardly go over it; it is but two fingers broad.' Piscator's companion was referring to the packhorse bridge known today as Viator's, at Milldale on the River Dove near Hartington, a popular terminus for walks through the Peak's most famous dale.

Ravenstor, Miller's Dale

The dramatic buttresses of Ravenstor in
Miller's Dale are lit by a declining autumn sun.
These towering white limestone cliffs, created
by the powerful meltwaters of Ice Age glaciers,
are popular with rock climbers who can often
be seen clinging to their minuscule holds like
flies on a wall.

Wallscape, Longdendale

Like sun-cracked mud in a desert pool, the
broken lines of drystone walls spread across
the rough moor grass of Longdendale in the far
north of the National Park. The tiny isolated
building in the bottom left of the photograph
is St James's Church, Woodhead, where many
of the navvies who died in the construction of
the Woodhead railway tunnels beneath the
Pennines in the 1840s, lie buried.

Trinnacle Stones, Saddleworth

The isolated gritstone pinnacles known as the
Trinnacle Stones overlook the wind-whipped
waters of the Greenfield Reservoir damming
Holme Clough, on the western slopes of Black
Hill (1,908 feet) in the north-west of the
National Park.

View from the Ladder

The sepia slopes of Grindslow Knoll (centre)
dominate this view of the valley of the River
Noe from the Jacob's Ladder footpath, a 'bad
weather alternative' to the Pennine Way.
Rushup Edge is in the background. Jacob's
Ladder got its name from Jacob Marshall, a
packhorse leader or 'jagger' who constructed
the original steps up to Edale Head in the
eighteenth century.

Autumn on Stanage

Fleeting autumn shadows flicker across the
golden bracken slopes below the grey gritstone
walls of Stanage Edge, one of the distinctive
Peakland edges which sweep like steps down
the eastern side of the Park. Stanage is a
favourite for rock climbers, with more than
five hundred routes recorded in its three-mile
length.

Nine Stones, Harthill Moor

Paradoxically named the Nine Stones, these four enigmatic monoliths on Harthill Moor near Birchover are among the most impressive of the Park's stone circles. Dated to the early Bronze Age, the circle may have connections with the burial ground on nearby Stanton Moor, which has its own stone circle called the Nine Ladies.

Riding the mist

The gritstone brow of Baslow Edge breaks through the autumnal mists rising from the Derwent Valley in this view from sunlit Froggatt Edge. These conditions of colder, heavier air in the valley bottom and sunny warmer conditions above are known to the meteorologist as 'temperature inversion', and are quite common in the Peak at this time of the year.

Autumn tapestry

One of the great glories of the Peakland
autumn is to walk through an old oak or beech
wood with the dying sunlight filtering through
the canopy of brilliantly coloured leaves. This
is Yarncliff Wood, Upper Padley, near
Grindleford.

Blowback, Kinder Downfall

A rainbow hovers fleetingly in the huge 'blow-back' of spray from the Peak's highest waterfall, the 100-foot Kinder Downfall, a landmark on the western edge of the 2,000-foot plateau. The unusual sight of a waterfall going uphill occurs when a strong westerly wind is funnelled up the valley of the Kinder River, pushing the water back in a dancing plume of spray.

WINTER

The Peak often features prominently in winter-time traffic news broadcasts, for roads like the notorious Snake Pass and the Woodhead trans-Pennine route further north are usually the first to close and the last to open when the snows come.

These warnings give an indication of the frequent severity of the Peak winter. It is hard to realize that the area is on the same latitude as Labrador or Siberia. Until, that is, blizzard conditions set in, and the modest heights of Kinder Scout and Bleaklow transform into frightening Arctic wildernesses.

Winter is the time when farming in the Peak becomes as much a test of endurance and survival as of husbandry, and the summer idylls of sun-kissed meadows are long forgotten. These extreme conditions breed a very special kind of farmer, able to accept and overcome almost anything that Nature can throw at him. And in winter, she usually does.

But there is a special kind of beauty, too, in the delicate wind-carved cornices of snow which overhang the edges, and in the ice-sheathed moorland grasses. When the sun does shine, the Peak can be transformed into an Alpine wonderland of glistening virginal snow slopes, dotted everywhere with the moving shapes of the moorland sheep.

Stormy day on Stanage

Storm clouds threaten from a lowering sky in
this winter view from Stanage Edge. Snow
dusts the distant view of Lose Hill (centre) and
Kinder Scout beyond, and hangs in the lee of
the ruler-straight enclosure walls in the
foreground, promising more to come.

Derbyshire Gritstones

The large, speckle-faced and hornless
Derbyshire Gritstone sheep were bred by local
shepherds to withstand the rigours of the Peak
climate. Originating in the Goyt Valley on the
western edge of the Park, they were first
known as the Dale o'Goyt until the Derbyshire
Gritstone Breed Society was formed at a
meeting in Bakewell in 1906. They are noted
for the fine quality of their wool, as well as for
their hardiness.

The church in the valley

A winter view of Holy Trinity Church, Edale,
which celebrated its centenary in 1985. The
village of Grindsbrook Booth (as Edale village
was formerly known) once had only a chapel
of ease, situated in the old churchyard, and the
dead had to be carried across the hill via
Hollins Cross to be buried in Castleton. The
later road link, via Mam Nick, is seen on the
skyline.

Snow shadows

There is a slight hint of warmer times to come, as the strengthening sun melts the last of the winter snows lingering in the shadow of the limestone walls in this photograph taken near Litton, looking towards Tansley and Peter's Dale.

A frosty morning on the Wye

A crisp, frosty winter's morning in the sheep-
cropped water meadows of the River Wye,
near Ashford-in-the-Water. A weak sun
gradually breaks through the mist rising off
the river and silhouettes the trees of Shacklow
Wood on the skyline.

Ground to a halt

A slightly surrealistic sight at Lawrence Field,
below Millstone Edge near Grindleford, are
these stacked piles of old millstones,
abandoned when cheaper alternatives flooded
the market in the late nineteenth century.
Millstone-making, using the eponymous
millstone grit, was once an important Peak
industry. The stones were used throughout the
country for anything from grinding corn to
sharpening the blades forged by the 'little
mesters' in Sheffield's cutlery industry.

Winter snows linger

The dark, snow-streaked mass of Seal Edge and
Fairbrook Naze on Kinder Scout are a
reminder of the severe conditions which exist
on the Peak's summit in winter, even when
sunlight adds a glow to the foreground
bracken slopes of Fair Brook. The view is from
the Snake Road near the Snake Inn, which
gives the pass its name.

Iced grasses

Even in the harshest winter there is beauty to
be found in the details of the Peak landscape.
Here, ice coats clough-side grasses in a frozen
envelope of transparent and transient
loveliness.

Trespass Route

It could be Labrador or Siberia and it is on the
same latitude, but in fact it is a mid-winter
scene on the Kinder Reservoir above Hayfield.
This was the route taken by the 1932 Mass
Trespassers on their protest march to gain the
right to roam on Kinder Scout, which resulted
in the imprisonment of five of the protesters.

Sun and snow on Stanage

Wind-sculptured cornices on Stanage Edge
lend an Alpine air to these modest heights,
especially when the sun breaks through,
adding subtlety in shade and shadow.

———————————————————————

Study in black and white

Snow-plastered trees and fences in Edale
provide a stark study in black and white,
simplifying the landscape to its basic
components. The only movement is provided
by the ubiquitous moorland sheep, for whom
the trees provide welcome shelter.

The essential Derwent

The essential Upper Derwent scene: a frieze of
naked birches in the foreground, the dark
band of conifers in the middle distance rising
to bracken and snow-covered high moors
behind. This is a mid-winter view from
Birchinlee across the reservoir-filled valley to
the Howden Moors beyond. It was on moors
like this that the sheepdog hero, Tip, stayed
with the dead body of its master for fifteen
weeks in 1954.

Kinder Downfall

The dramatic view from the lip of Kinder
Downfall in 'blow-back' conditions. The peaty,
whisky-gold waters of the Kinder River are
blown back in a curtain of shifting spray over
the glistening rocks, while the watery eye of
the Kinder Reservoir glints in the broad green
valley below.

Ice cave on Kinder

The winter walker on Kinder Scout is
sometimes treated to some extraordinary
sights, like this ice cave which forms in the
right conditions behind the frozen 100-foot
cascade of Kinder Downfall. Icicles hang like
stalactites from the frozen rocks creating a
translucent ice palace, and a convenient
shelter from the freezing wind for the passing
rambler.

In winter's icy grip

A solitary tree, frozen in the grip of its winter
sleep, awaits the call of spring high on the
snow-clad White Peak plateau near Monyash.
The silhouetted shelter belt in the middle
distance follows the line of an old lead-mining
rake, planted to keep cattle out from the
poisoned and dangerous ground as well as to
give them shelter from the icy winds.

Farming at the edge

Edgetop Farm, near Crowdicote in the upper
Dove Valley, basks in the brief winter sun,
sheltered by its belt of beeches and watched
over by the Matterhorn-like fang of Parkhouse
Hill (centre left). This photograph gives some
impression of the harshness of the farmer's life
in the depths of a Peakland winter, when the
elemental forces of nature still dictate any
activity out of doors.

Coniferous gloom

The monotonous, lifeless interior of a larch
plantation is a desert as far as native wildlife
is concerned, and the National Park authority
has tried to discourage this kind of blanket
afforestation in the Peak. Many such
plantations still remain, however, and the
Forestry Commission and others now pursue
more enlightened planting policies, favouring
native, broadleaved species.

Below Stanage

Overstones Farm nestles below the escarpment
of Stanage Edge at more than 1,000 feet above
sea level, commanding extensive views south
down the Derwent Valley and north to Win
Hill (centre distance) and the enclosure fields
of Carrhead. Kinder Scout and the Derwent
Moors form the backdrop.

Ice and stone

This ice-encrusted gritstone wall is a testament
to the ferocity of the Peakland winter, as wind-
blown ice provides a temporary 'mortar' for
the drystone construction.

Sunset from Kinder

Sunbeams light a pastel landscape seen from
Kinder Downfall, looking west towards
Stockport and Manchester, from where so
many of the Park's eighteen and a half million
annual visitors come.